GORILLAS

A TRUE BOOK

by

Patricia A. Fink Martin

Children's Press®
A Division of Grolier Publishing

New York London Hong Kong Sydney
Danbury, Connecticut

A baby gorilla

Reading Consultant
Linda Cornwell
*Coordinator of School Quality
and Professional Improvement
Indiana State Teachers Association*

Content Consultant
Kathy Carlstead, Ph.D.
*National Zoological Park
Washington, D.C.*

The photographs on the cover and
title page show male mountain
gorillas in forests in East Africa.

Visit Children's Press® on the Internet at:
http://publishing.grolier.com

Library of Congress Cataloging-in-Publication Data

Martin, Patricia A. Fink, 1955–
    Gorillas / by Patricia A. Fink Martin.
        p. cm. — (A true book)
    Includes bibliographical references and index.
    Summary: Describes the physical characteristics, habitat, life cycle, and
behavior of the gorilla.
    ISBN: 0-516-21570-1 (lib. bdg.)   0-516-27014-1 (pbk.)
    1. Gorilla—Juvenile literature. [1. Gorilla.] I. Title. II. Series.
QL737.P96M375 2000
599.884—dc21
                                                                99-17067
                                                                    CIP
                                                                    AC

Contents

Man-Eating Monster
or Gentle Giant?   5

The Biggest Primate   11

Gorilla Families   18

A Gorilla Day   28

Gorillas in Danger   39

To Find Out More   44

Important Words   46

Index   47

Meet the Author   48

Sometimes gorillas can look scary.

Man-Eating Monster or Gentle Giant?

When you were younger, were you afraid of monsters? Did they hide under your bed? Did they live in your closet? What did they look like? Were they big and hairy?

This young gorilla is eating a plant.

Gorillas are big and hairy with dark fur. They live in Africa. In the past, some people thought they were monsters. Some even said that gorillas eat people.

Today we know that gorillas do not eat people. In the wild, they do not even eat meat. They eat plants.

Gorillas are not monsters, but they are huge, powerful animals. The males are much

An adult male gorilla is a huge animal.

larger than the females. Male gorillas weigh up to 400 pounds (182 kilograms). They have big, broad shoulders and long, thick arms. Sometimes they stand up on two legs. They are as tall as most men and twice as heavy.

Gorillas have big teeth and jaws. They need them to eat tough leaves and stems. Strong muscles open and close their jaws. These thick muscles extend to the top of

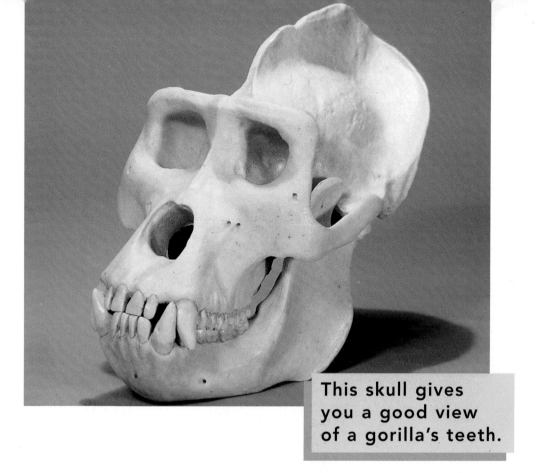

This skull gives you a good view of a gorilla's teeth.

their heads! If you live near a zoo, go there and watch a gorilla chew. You will see the fur on its head wrinkle and wriggle. Beneath the skin, the muscles are working hard.

Gorillas are primates. Monkeys and people are primates too.

The Biggest Primate

Gorillas belong to a group of animals called mammals. Mice, cats, whales, and bats are also mammals. Scientists place gorillas in a group of mammals called primates. Monkeys are primates too, and so are humans. The gorilla is the largest of all primates alive

A chimpanzee (above) and an orangutan (right) are great apes.

12

today. Gorillas are also members of a group called the great apes. Chimpanzees, orangutans, and bonobos are great apes too. The great apes are all large primates that have no tails.

Like most primates, gorillas are curious and smart. Their eyes are close together in the front of their heads, so they can tell whether objects are nearby or far away.

Would you hold hands with a gorilla? What would it feel like? Gorilla hands are big, but they are shaped like ours. Their skin is smooth and tough, so it feels like a person wearing leather gloves. Gorillas have four long fingers and a thumb, so they can pick up and hold small objects. Each finger has a flat fingernail at its end.

Can you imagine holding
a gorilla's hand?

15

Three Kinds

Scientists recognize three kinds of gorillas. The western lowland gorilla is the most common kind of gorilla. This small gorilla lives in the forests of western Africa. It has a coat of short dark fur. A cap of grayish brown fur sits on top of its head. Have you ever seen a gorilla at the zoo? Almost all zoo gorillas are from west Africa.

The eastern lowland gorilla lives in the rain forest of central Africa. It is larger than the western gorilla. Short black fur covers most of its body.

A western lowland gorilla

# of Gorillas

The mountain gorilla is found in a tiny area of east Africa. This large gorilla lives in meadows and forests on the slopes of what were once volcanoes. Its home is cold and damp, but its thick long hair keeps the mountain gorilla warm.

A mountain gorilla

An eastern lowland gorilla

Gorilla Families

The three kinds of gorillas are alike in many ways. All gorillas are born into a gorilla troop. A troop is a kind of family. Most troops have ten to thirty members. Many gorillas in a troop are related. A young gorilla may have an older sister or brother, a half-

A gorilla troop is like a big family. Each troop has one adult male, several females, some young males, and babies.

brother or a half-sister, or an uncle. Of course, it has a mother and a father too.

The father is the head of the family. He is a large adult

Every troop of gorillas is led by an adult male silverback.

male between 15 and 45
years old. Silver gray hair
covers his broad back.
Because he has a silvery coat,

he is called a silverback. Younger males also live in the troop. They are not quite adults, so their hair has not yet turned silver. They are called blackbacks. The black-backs act as lookouts and guards.

The rest of the troop is made up of youngsters and adult females. Some of them have young. Some do not. Like humans, gorillas take a long time to grow up.

This newborn gorilla is sleeping on its mother's back.

Young gorillas are loved by every gorilla in the troop. When a gorilla is born, all the other gorillas want to see it. Gorillas are born without much hair. Their skin is pinkish gray. They are very small at first. How much did you weigh when you were born?

At birth, a gorilla weighs only about 4 pounds (1.8 kilograms). For the first few months, the mother gorilla cradles the baby against her chest. She feeds it

A mother gorilla cradles her baby to keep it warm and safe.

Young gorillas cannot walk very far. When the troop moves, a young gorilla must ride on its mother's back.

milk. When the family travels, the mother walks slowly while the baby clings to the hairs on her stomach. When the young gorilla is older, it will ride on her back.

A gorilla family

Gorillas keep growing until they are 8 to 10 years old. In any gorilla troop, there may be several youngsters. Just like human children, young gorillas love to play. Most of their day is spent playing.

Gorillas do not have playgrounds to play in, but the silverback's large back makes a perfect slide. Sliding down a tree trunk or a twisting vine

Young gorillas love to play. This 1-year-old baby is playing with a 9-year-old male.

A young mountain gorilla is climbing up a vine.

can be fun too. Young gorillas also like to swing on trees and vines in the forest. When young gorillas are on the ground, they chase one another around the trees. A hill is a great place to roll and tumble.

A Gorilla Day

A gorilla family eats, travels, and sleeps together. Their day begins as the sun rises. One by one, the gorillas wake up. They yawn and stretch. Then they sit up and look around. Gorillas may build their nests on the ground or up in a tree.

This nest was built by a gorilla.

The gorillas are hungry. They begin to search for food. It does not take long to find something to eat. As the gorillas eat, they make little noises. What sounds do you

These gorillas
are eating tree
bark (above).
An eastern
lowland gorilla
munches on
bamboo (right).

make when something tastes good? You might say, "mmmh mmmh." Gorillas say "naoom, naoom." It sounds like they are clearing their throats.

Most gorillas eat the leaves and stems that grow on the ground. Mountain gorillas like wild celery and bamboo. They love blackberries. They also eat snails and small insects.

A few hours later, the gorillas are full. They nap for a while. While the adults rest,

Gorillas often rest in the afternoon.

the young ones play. By afternoon, it is time to move on.
The group walks slowly
through the tall grass. They
walk on all fours with their
feet flat on the ground. They
hold the palms of their hands

When gorillas walk, they hold the palms of their hands off the ground.

up off the ground. Their weight rests on their knuckles and bent fingers. As gorillas move, they grunt softly. Sometimes they stop to feed.

When the sun goes down, the troop stops for the night. Each gorilla makes a new bed

A mother mountain gorilla shares her nest with her baby.

of stems and leaves. Very young gorillas share their mother's nest. Scattered about, the gorillas sleep.

Nearby, the silverback rests too. All day he has led the group. He led them to a place to eat. He decided when to move on. He chose the night's resting place. Even as he sleeps, he is ready to protect the group.

At the faintest sound, he jumps to his feet. He stares

This silverback is looking for food.

and begins to hoot loudly.
Rising up on two legs, he
cups his hands and drums on
his chest. This makes a hollow
pok-pok-pok sound. He rushes madly around in a circle.

This gorilla hoots loudly and beats his chest when he senses danger.

As he runs, he whacks at the plants and thumps on the ground. Then he charges. Roaring, he rushes through the brush.

The silverback puts on a terrifying show, but he is quite gentle with his family. He loves youngsters. Picking one off its mother's stomach, he strokes its hair. He picks out burrs and insects. Then he hands the young gorilla back to its mother.

Gorillas in Danger

Young gorillas are well guarded by the silverback and other adult gorillas. The adults will die to defend young gorillas from danger. At one time, leopards and lions were a gorilla's worst enemy, but today it is humans. It is against the law to hunt and

39

This mountain gorilla was killed by hunters.

kill gorillas, but some people
do it anyway.

People also cut down their
forests to grow crops and
herd cattle. When we destroy

If we destroy the forest where gorillas live, how will they survive?

the land where gorillas live, where can they go? All gorillas are in danger today, but only the mountain gorilla is an endangered species. It has

Gorillas are special animals.
We should try to save them.

been placed on a list of the rarest animals in the world. There are fewer than seven hundred mountain gorillas left on Earth.

You can help the gorillas by joining a group that protects wild animals. Start a school project to earn money. Give the money to take care of young gorillas that have lost their mothers. Only with our help will these gentle giants survive.

To Find Out More

If you would like to learn more about gorillas, check out these additional resources.

 **Books**

Demuth, Patricia. *Gorillas*. Putnam Publishing Group, 1994.

Murray, Peter. *Gorillas*. Childs World, 1994.

Patterson, Francine. *Koko's Kitten*. Scholastic, Inc., 1985.

Redmond, Ian. *Gorilla*. Alfred A. Knopf, 1995.

Woods, Mae. *Gorillas*. Abdo & Daughters, 1997.

Videos
Twilight of the Gorilla. American Adventure Productions, Inc.; MPI Home Video, 1988, 1991.

Gorilla. National Geographic Society, Washington, D.C., 1992.

Gorillas in the Mist. MCA Homevideo, Inc., 1989.

💡 Organizations and Online Sites

The Dian Fossey Gorilla Fund International
Adopt-a-Gorilla Program
800 Cherokee Ave., SE
Atlanta, GA 30315
http://www.gorillafund.org

The Gorilla Foundation
P.O. Box 620-640
Woodside, CA 94062-9901
http://www.gorilla.org/

Gorilla Haven
*http://www.
gorilla-haven.org/*

This site has ideas for
reports on gorillas and all
kinds of fun facts and
photographs.

International Primate Protection League
P.O. Box 766
Summerville, SC 29484
http://www.ippl.org

Rainforest Action Network
221 Pine Street, Suite 500
San Francisco, CA 94104
415-398-4404
http://www.ran.org

Important Words

endangered species a type of living thing in danger of dying out

great ape a large primate without a tail, such as the chimpanzee, the gorilla, the orangutan, and the bonobo, very closely related to humans

mammal a group of vertebrates (animals with backbones) that have fur, are warm-blooded, and produce milk for their young

primate a type of mammal with hands that grasp, eyes set close together in the front of the face, and a large brain

volcano a cone-shaped hill or mountain with a central opening. If the volcano is active, lava occasionally erupts out of the opening.

Index

blackbacks, 21
bonobo, 13, 46
brains, 13, 46
chimpanzee, **12**, 13, 46
day, typical, 28–38
eastern lowland gorilla,
    16, **17**, 18, **30**
endangered species, 40,
    41, **42**, 43, 46
eyes, 13, 46
families, 18–27, **25**, 28
food, **6**, 7, 8, 29, **30**, 31,
    35, **36**
great apes, 11–13, 46
habitat, 16, 17, 40, **41**
hands, 14, **15**, 46
humans, **10**, 11, 39, 40,
    40, 46
mammal, 11, 46
monkey, **10**, 11
mountain gorilla, 1, 17,
    17, 18, **27**, **34**, **40**, 41

nest, 28, **29**, **34**, 35
orangutan, **12**, 13, 46
play, 25-27, **26**, 32
primate, **10**, 11–13, **12**,
    46
protection, 35–39, **37**
rest, 31, **32**, 35
silverback, 20, **20**, 21,
    26, 35, **36**, 38, 39
size, 7, **7**, 8
strength, 8, 9
teeth, 8, 9, **9**
troop, 18, **19**, **20**, 21, **24**,
    25
volcano, 17, 46
walking, 32, 33, **33**
western lowland gorilla,
    16, **16**, 18
zoo gorilla, 16

Meet the Author

Patricia A. Fink Martin has a doctorate in biology. After working in the laboratory and teaching for 10 years, she began writing science books for children. *Booklist* chose her first book, *Animals that Walk on Water*, as one of the ten best animal books for children in 1998. Dr. Martin lives in Tennessee with her husband, Jerry, and their daughter, Leslie.